CHILD-AND-ROSE

The Poet Aygi by Genadii Gogoliuk
(Oil on Canvas, 71 x 56 cm)
Photo Courtesy of John Martin Gallery, London

CHILD-AND-ROSE

GENNADY AYGI

**Translated from the Russian by
PETER FRANCE**

Preface by BEI DAO

A NEW DIRECTIONS BOOK

ACKNOWLEDGMENTS

Various parts of this volume appeared earlier in the following publications:
Veronica's Book (an earlier, less complete version) and "Sleep-And-Poetry": Polygon Books, Edinburgh (1989). "Leaf-fall and Silence," "Snow at Midday," "Two Epilogues" and eight poems from *Veronica's Book* in *Gennady Aygi: Selected Poems 1954-94*: Angel Books, London / Hydra Books (Northwestern University Press), Evanston, IL (1997). "Poetry-As-Silence" in *Southfields*, Glasgow (1997). The Foreword is in part an adaptation of an article entitled "Gennadii Aigi: Modernity and Community," published in *Mantis* (Stanford, CA), I, 63-71.

Book design by Sylvia Frezzolini Severance
Manufactured in the United States of America
New Directions Books are printed on acid-free paper.
First published as a New Directions Paperbook Original (NDP 954) in 2003
Published simultaneously in Canada by Penguin Books Canada Limited

Library of Congress Cataloging-in-Publication Data

Aygi, Gennady, 1934-
  [Poems. English. Selections]
  Child-And-Rose / Gennady Aygi ; translated from the Russian by
Peter France; preface by Bei Dao.
    p. cm.
  ISBN 0-8112-1536-9 (alk. paper)
  1. Aygi, Gennady, 1934 - Translations into English.
  I. France, Peter, 1935– II. Title.
  PG3478.I35 A24 2003
  891.71'44—dc21   2002151607

New Directions Books are published for James Laughlin
by New Directions Publishing Corporation
80 Eighth Avenue, New York, NY 10011

CONTENTS

PREFACE

In June of 1992 I met Gennady Aygi at the Rotterdam International Poetry Festival. Besides organizing poetry readings, this festival has a tradition of inviting participants to take part in a workshop where the poetry of one contemporary poet is translated into various languages. That year Aygi's work was chosen. The Chinese poet Song Ling and a Dutch sinologist attended the workshop each morning, bringing in their Chinese translations of Aygi's poems one after another. The utterly unique, unusual style of his poetry shocked me. I immediately asked another Chinese poet to interview Aygi and published this along with nine of his poems translated by Song Ling in that year's third issue of the literary journal, *Today*, where I am the editor-in-chief. For the first time, Aygi's poems were available to Chinese readers.

Later the same summer, Aygi and I lectured at a school for writers in Copenhagen. One evening, we went to a bar and drank until midnight. The conversation was illuminating – he was sociable, sensitive, and full of insight. To converse with a poet while drinking provides an alternate understanding of the poet's writing.

In an essay I once described a number of golden chains that exist in twentieth century world poetry. Concerning the golden chain of Russian poetry, I mentioned three names: Mandelstam, Pasternak, and Aygi. Though this golden chain should perhaps include others, these three voices are for me the most innovative and original. Each complements the other in a perfect bond between a spirit of humanity that has both endured great suffering and can also turn stone into gold.

As a student of the Gorky Literary Institute towards the end of the 1950s, Aygi was a neighbor of Pasternak's – who had just received the Nobel Prize and was under attack – and they eventually became close friends despite a great difference in age. It was Pasternak who encouraged Aygi to begin writing in Russian, forging together two links of this golden chain. As a result, Aygi was expelled from the Gorky Literary Institute and drifted around Moscow without a residence permit or money, at times forced to spend the night in subway stations. Practically unknown to the Russian public until the 1980s, his writing was also forced underground.

Aygi was born in 1934 in a southern village of the Chuvash Republic. He grew up in this remote place; both Moscow and St. Petersburg are some five hundred miles away. His mother tongue is Chuvash. The source of his poetic spirit arises from Chuvash folk songs that trace back to the vast, hidden folds of ancient religions and legends. A child of the Chuvash countryside arrives in Moscow, taking what verges on an ancient culture into the poetry of Russian and European modernism, fusing them together. Perhaps it can be said that at this point Russian poetry escaped from a cruel never-ending forest of oppression, delved deep into the hinterland, concealing its talents and waiting for the right moment to emerge again.

Literature is an ideology at the forefront of resistance, often transforming official discourse into a kind of echo. Distinct from most other literary works, Aygi's poems arise from the interior of language to effect its subversion as if removing the firewood beneath a boiling kettle. His intention is to break open the system of rhymes and the linguistic train of traditional Russian poetry as a way to achieve a powerful new system of prosody. In an interview he once gave for *Today*, he said: "An autocratic ideology always wants to pursue systemization as a kind of assimilation and makes each word wear a solid body of armor. . . . From another perspective it can be said that the use of rhyme is like playing chess. Despite the continuously changing moves in chess, when a limit's reached there's only repetition. A poem's musical rhythm and prosody flow naturally from within its compositional demands – given time – which then allows the shape of such things to become a revolt of meanings. Generally speaking, prosody always fetters thought, and is against freedom." Reading Aygi's poetry can be a kind of adventure. His poems contain a special code consisting of precise diction, phrase structure, broken lines, intervals of space, and punctuation marks. Readers must break the code in order to truly enter his poetry.

In the spring of 1994, I received a letter of invitation from the Chuvash Republic, inquiring if I could attend the festivities for the sixtieth birthday celebration of their national poet, Aygi. Regrettably, I was unable to go. Nearly ten years later, Aygi's poems display an even greater vitality that is unique among his peers. Against the apparent pretences of a postmodern landscape, he uses his poems as a testament: love and faith are our ever-present roots, our source of life.

Bei Dao
2002 October 5
Beloit, Wisconsin

(Translated from the Chinese by Jeffrey Yang)

FOREWORD

GENNADY AYGI, born in 1934 in southern Chuvashia, is now, after years of harassment, recognized as the Chuvash national poet. At the same time, he occupies a central place in what could be called – though he does not like the term – the Russian and European poetic avant-garde. This double identity is not without its problems. By way of introducing his poetry to the American reader, I will offer here some thoughts on a difficult poem of 1989, "The Circle," which explores the relations of community and modernity.

First, some of Aygi's own history and that of his people. The Chuvash Republic is a small territory of some two million inhabitants on the right bank of the Volga, where the river makes its great bend southwards towards the Caspian Sea. Today, it is part of the Russian Federation, and it has been ruled from Moscow or St. Petersburg since the time of Ivan the Terrible, but its population is not predominantly Russian or even Slav. The Chuvash are a people of complex origins, claiming descent from the Huns and Bulgars among others, speaking a Turkic language, and still preserving – in the face of modernization and industrialization – many vestiges of their old rural culture. Until the forced conversions of the eighteenth and nineteenth centuries, this ancestral culture was a pagan one, with a religion stressing the sanctity of communal life and the bonds between humanity and the natural world. It found expression in chants, riddles, festivals, and, perhaps most strongly, in the *khorovod* or choral dance.

By the time the future national poet was growing up in the 1940s, this traditional life had taken a battering, not only from the Revolution, but also from collectivization and World War II (in which Aygi's father died). The young poet's relations with the world of his ancestors were problematic. On the one hand, his mother, who came from a lineage of pagan priests, represented – and still represents – for him the sacred values of his people; on the other,

Mayakovsky, discovered in his teens, was a powerful emblem of poetic modernity. Encouraged by Peder Khuzangay, one of the principal Chuvash poets and the father of the dedicatee of "The Circle," Aygi left his native land to study at the Literary Institute in Moscow. This led to the discovery of Baudelaire, Nietzsche and Kafka, but also to friendship with Boris Pasternak, his neighbor in the writers' colony of Peredelkino. At this time he still wrote his poems in Chuvash, but Pasternak and the Turkish poet Nazim Hikmet (then living in exile in Moscow) urged him to write in Russian, plugging his writing directly into modern European literature. The year 1960 brought the deaths of both Pasternak and Aygi's mother — significantly, the very first poem he wrote directly in Russian is the beautiful lyric, "Death," which begins:

> Not taking the scarf from her head
> mother is dying.

So the twenty-five-year-old poet now belonged to Russian and European culture. At the same time, his friendship with Pasternak, together with his unorthodox way of writing, led to harassment, and this was naturally more intense in the relatively small Chuvash community. A *persona non grata* at home, he found a second home in the rootless, adventurous Moscow "underground" of poets, painters, and musicians, and soon found work in the Mayakovsky Museum, where he became an expert on the revolutionary Russian art of the early twentieth century. A far cry from Chuvashia, it might seem.

Yet his native culture was not forgotten. For many years he could not return home, but Chuvash themes — field and forest, both richly symbolic — permeated his writing. He avoided the "folkloric" (it was all too easy for a Soviet writer from one of the small nationalities of the Union to trade in local color), but he remained true to the ethical and aesthetic principles of Chuvash culture, above all the solidarity among people and with the natural world. In 1969-70 he wrote: "First of all, it [my debt to Chuvash culture] has been visible in the fact that for me poetry is always that kind of 'action' and 'connection' which is best expressed by the word *svyashchennodeistvie* [sacred act]." It was this high seriousness, alongside his startlingly original work with words, that increasingly attracted readers and translators from abroad. Before long, he became better known and certainly more appreciated in Europe at large than in Russia or Chuvashia.

His own poetry, damned as cosmopolitan, could not be published in the Soviet Union, but he could still obtain commissions to translate into Chuvash. In this way, he made a vital contribution to his native culture. In 1969 he published a remarkable anthology of French poetry in Chuvash, from Villon to Bonnefoy, and including many modern poets; this had a liberating effect on Chuvash poetry, opening up undreamed-of possibilities, both formal and thematic. At the same time, he was involving himself with Chuvash culture from another angle; his anthology of texts from the old pagan chants and prayers to the sometimes tragic poetry of the Soviet period was designed to allow the "Chuvash word" to resound in France and all over the world. (In fact, the first translation of the anthology came out in Italy in the 1980s, followed a few years later by my English translation, *An Anthology of Chuvash Poetry*.)

The Gorbachev years altered the situation radically. After long years in the wilderness, Aygi was welcomed back as a public figure in his homeland in the late 1980s, eventually becoming the national poet, winning prizes and honors, and being proclaimed a "second cosmonaut" (the first being modern Chuvashia's most famous son, the cosmonaut Nikolaev). He began to spend more time in his homeland, playing a key part in the cultural life of the nation and reflecting more and more on the relationship of an uprooted, modern, cosmopolitan poet with the world of his ancestors. It is to this period of renewed contact that "The Circle" belongs. It was written in 1989 and first published in his Russian-language collection *Now There Are Always Snows* (1992).

Круг

Атнеру Хузангаю

время — одно — лишь одно: говорить о простом
повторяясь пылающим кругом! —

и как будто восходит заря — расширяя крестьянские
празднества
и вытягивая — до садовых вершин
блекло-алую память о платьях — давно отшуршавших:

свет — все алее — из далей забвенья! —

о зори — закаты — о годы-сиянья — сиянья-века! — как
знамена-и-знаменья:

Целомудрия — Верности — Силы! —

а теперь уже — долго-далекого плача:

по народо-корням-человекам! — и ответно сияют
сыновье-и-отче-сиянья

во-Родине — будто на дереве-вещи — на хлебе-мерцании
центра! — и в зареве — в заревах
почво-горенья от рук:

снова — страда пониманья: восходят-плывут по-над
полем

кони-движенья все ярче как раны —

вещь из соломы поет на весь мир — и повозка в луну
углубляется! вечностью
золото мозга пылает —

(где-то возводится сруб
и общаются звонкостью звона

братски-понятные бревна — со смыслогорением
в глухих от счастья плечах) —

золото мозга пылает
здесь — среди букв: как в волненьи дыханья —
    отцовско-сыновьего: властью и трепетом свежим:

в мире — живого-меня! —

знаю — что даже прощаться придут — словно с даром
    последним — с вещами-строгать: с породненным
    железом священно-привычным для резанья
                        грустно-родного —

сразу же — здесь — отсиять заставляя
древоодежду мою — до братанья: с Землею

More than many of Aygi's poems, this one is difficult to interpret. Often, in translating his work, I have discussed meaning with him, but in the end the responsibility is the translator's. The version given below is as accurate as possible, though it resolves certain ambiguities which should remain unresolved. I have been guided by a long acquaintance with the poet's work and have tried to suggest the rhythms of the original.

The Circle

to Atner Khuzangay

time – one time – just one: to speak of the simple
repeating itself in a flaming circle! –

and dawn seems to break – expanding village feastdays
and stretching – to the tops of gardens
faded-scarlet memory of dresses – long rustled-away:

light – ever more scarlet – from far places of forgetting! –

oh dayglow – oh sunsets – oh years-of-shining – century-shining! – like
signs-and-signals:

of Modesty – Loyalty – Strength! –

but now already – of prolonged-far-off weeping:

for tribal-root-people! – and there shine in reply son-and-father
shinings
in-Motherland – as if on a tree-thing – on corn-gleam of the center! – in
the glow – in the skyglow

of soil-burning from hands:

and again – the work of understanding: up-over the field swim-soar
movement-horses ever brighter like wounds –

a thing of straw to the whole world sings – and a cart plunges into
the moon! with eternity
gold flames in the brain –

(somewhere a log-hut is rising
and the logs with brotherly clarity
commune in clamorous chatter – with speaking-of-sense
in shoulders sonorous with happiness)

gold flames in the brain
here – amid letters: as in the emotion of breathing – of fathers-and-
sons: with power and trembling freshness:

in the world – of myself-alive! –

I know – they will even come and will part – as if with a final gift –
with things-for-planing: with connected iron sacredly-
familiar for sadly-intimate cutting –
here – straight away – making my treeclothing fade –
before brotherhood is sworn with Earth

The poem is dedicated to Atner Petrovich Khuzangay, a close friend of the poet and an important figure in modern Chuvash culture. He is a linguist, a scholar and a critic, but also a politician. As the first president of the Chuvash National Convention, he was particularly concerned with questions of cultural identity, the emblems of nationhood, and above all the fate of the Chuvash language. His presence in the poem represents perhaps the hope for a future that will keep the ancient traditions alive – or at least the awareness of what has vanished, and what may yet be lost.

I do not wish to comment at length on the text of Aygi's poem. Much could be said, for instance, about the sonorities and rhythms, the latter in particular carrying a powerful semantic or thematic weight. When Aygi reads his poems aloud, you are conscious of the strong tonic beat running through the verse – often in ternary meter, as in the opening lines here. The rhythm is by no means regular and there are no rhymes, but even so this "free verse" is an incantation (Aygi has been seen as a shamanistic figure). It is like the beat of the choral dance which still persists in Chuvashia, the embodiment of community, and a central theme of the poem. Yet at the same time the reader, as opposed to the listener, is struck by the fragmentary feel of the text, accentuated by unusual punctuation and typography, with varying line-lengths and eye-catching white spaces. It is as if two poems were vying for dominance, the chant or dance heard by the listener in the common space, and the broken modern text seen by the solitary reader. And in a way that is what the poem is about: the solitary poet's place in the "circle."

There are echoes here of many of Aygi's poems of all periods, but particularly those of the 1980s, when he dwelt on the relation between the modern poet, living in a wider world, and the traditional peasant world symbolized by ritual song and dance. From 1988 to 1991, before and after "The Circle," he wrote a collection of beautiful quatrains (there have been more since) under the title *Salute – to Singing* (available in a bilingual edition by Zephyr Books, 2002). These jewel-like poems are variations on themes from Chuvash and Tatar folk songs, often echoing the texts collected in

Aygi's Chuvash anthology. The speaker alternates between a "we," the dancers:

> Enough, we have swung and swung
> like ringing silver coins,
> we shall bow, shall bend before you
> like paper money, all white

and an "I" who looks back on the dance from a place outside:

> There's no way to still my pain,
> half my soul remains in that field!
> I say nothing, but beyond the hill like a child
> a marten weeps out loud.

There is no remedy for this division of the self: the westernized poet may re-enter the community imaginatively, but remains apart. So it is in "The Circle."

The dominant images conjured up in this fragmented poem are those of an ancient dance, associated with fire, light and redness (the red of festive peasant costumes). These are images of wholeness which emerge from the distance and the depths of memory, like a dawn breaking. They are connected with the ongoing community: fathers-and-sons, welded into a single word, in the Motherland. It is a community of work, ideally symbolized by the common building of a log hut, in which the natural, vegetable world is transformed by labor in field, garden and forest. The "tree-thing" (i.e. the material-ity of the tree), which figures in the middle of the poem alongside the grain in the field, is echoed at the end in the archaic *drevo-* of the invented compound word *drevoodezhda* (treeclothing); in the Chuvash worldview, the tree often has a sacred function, the *kiremet* or solitary tree being a place of ritual gathering.

At the end of the poem, this "treeclothing" is doomed to fade. The shining freshness of the dancing circle exists primarily in the memory. This is a poem of loss and parting. At the same time, however, we may be reminded of the vision of Aygi's mentor, Pasternak, who in *Doctor Zhivago* writes about the way in which art continually asserts life by confronting death. Here, then, the vanished world of community is resurrected in the action of poetry. The poet is not simply reflecting nostalgically on what he has lost; he is offering his readers a poem that imaginatively reasserts their common heritage.

Of course there is a paradox here. The poet writes of the common experience, but in a language far removed from the common language. Mallarmé, with whom Aygi was compared by the French writer and man of the theater, Antoine Vitez, saw the poet's role as being to "purify" the "language of the tribe." This purification seems necessarily to involve a certain hermeticism – and indeed "hermetic" is one of the labels applied to Aygi's poetry by Russian critics. It is not so much that he uses out-of-the-way words or allusions – his neologisms are easily comprehensible – as that his adventurously elliptical and ambiguous syntax means that his poems are far removed from straightforward prose statements. How can a poem about community be so remote from the actual community it celebrates?

Perhaps we should not exaggerate the difficulty. Research done in Chuvash schools suggests that quite young children, rather than searching for a translatable meaning, can respond imaginatively to the stimulus of this poetry. Or again, we might remember Pasternak's "unheard-of simplicity," which is less the apparent simplicity of the familiar and banal than the challenging simplicity of a new personal vision. If the reader is not constantly seeking to explain the poem, to restate it in prose, it can make its impact directly through its sounds, rhythms and images. In this, Aygi's work is at one with much of the best modern poetry.

Even so, "The Circle" is difficult in that it gives voice to the difficulty of living in a divided world. It seems to spring from the desire for an impossible relationship, for a return to the uncomplicated communal world of the ancestors, where the poet/singer is the direct voice of the people, and as such is immediately understood and adopted by them. Aygi, by contrast, only achieved recognition as a voice of the nation by way of a complicated itinerary, a parabolic journey through the literary world of modern Europe. He could perhaps be compared to Jean-Jacques Rousseau, the "citizen of Geneva," but an absent citizen who lived away from his homeland, for only by doing so could he speak for what he saw as its true values. So Aygi, while voicing the tragic fragmentation of his — and our — world, attempts to keep faith with the Chuvash community, prolonging its traditional culture by means that would have seemed quite foreign to it. As we have seen, the circle dance continues in the rhythm of his poem, even if the vision of it is shattered in vivid fragments of image.

At the same time, in the writing of poetry, a new community is forged, albeit a potential community. It includes in the first place the dedicatee, Khuzangay, for Aygi's poems are often addressed to individuals. But they are addressed too to other, unknown readers, like his "poem" entitled "Pages of Friendship," which invites the reader to pick a blade of grass and press it between the pages. So in Chuvashia, in Russia, and throughout the world, readers whose experience may be far remote from that of the poet can enter into the vision of togetherness and separation. They too can join the circle.

•

I have been lucky enough to be part of that circle for nearly thirty years now. An essential part of my friendship with Gennady Aygi has been the translation of much of his poetry, originally done with no thought of publication. In the days when communication was more difficult, translation was like a long-distance conversation between Britain and Russia.

The present volume brings together poetry and prose. The prose texts, poetic in their own right, are reflections on two of Aygi's central themes, sleep and silence, in their relation to poetic creation. The poems include the second, augmented edition of a collection first published in English by Polygon, Edinburgh, in 1989, *Veronica's Book* — poems inspired by the birth of Aygi's only daughter (he has five sons) – together with other poems on related themes, mostly published here for the first time in English, and a distinctive little work, *Silvia's World*, written for a small girl in Paris whose room was lent to Aygi during a visit to France in 1991.

Childhood is indeed at the heart of this collection, so it seems fitting to conclude this foreword with a text taken from an interview given by Aygi to a Yugoslavian journal in 1985, in which he talks about poetry and childhood:

Perhaps in contemporary poetry we need to approach childhood-as-being not only in terms of "heart-and-feeling," but also as a matter of principle. It's not just a question of our need for that remembered "freshness of impressions." In childhood we trusted the world more – it stood open to us, and was for us a veritable world-Universum.

We should do well to remember this. For in our *perception of the world* (not our knowledge) we have shrunk the world-as-universe to an incredible degree, turning it into a little bazaar-world – no wider than "orbits round earth." Isn't it true that precisely in this "cosmic age" we have less and less feeling for *universality*, for the World-as-Universum? This little world of earthly fear and fears ... do we really experience anything beyond this?

So let us not be condescending to the being-of-childhood, enraptured as it is by the miracle of the existence of the inexplicably-meaningful world (much in nature itself shows that it was not created for man alone).

The "theme of childhood" today can be more than simply nostalgic, it can raise "theoretical problems" for contemporary poetry. For example, in spite of all our knowledge (very paradoxically in this "age of knowledge") we live and have our being in a strange atmosphere.... For us creation is finished and dead, in it there is no continuing manifestation of the creative force, but the anonymous "laws of the universe," as if "given" once and for all – everything is geared to the world's being experienced as finished (once again, I am speaking here not of knowledge, but of the *perception of the world*) – what room is there for poetry to "soar" here? – and yet, I tell myself, I haven't lost everything if with my one-time child-self I can recall that once something reached me that was more distant than the light embodied merely in the sun which stood above the village.

I have also my "personal" reason for returning to my childhood in thought-and-poetry. Even the human world which I saw *then*, connected as it is with those distant impressions, was nobler than what I have met with since. I don't think this is just idealization. It was a world of truly patient people, people of "village and field," their greatest beauty being the minimum of work needed for today and tomorrow. – I lived in a world where the human imagination (and this is perhaps the very thing of whose creation it is said that it was made "in His own image"), yes, I lived in a world where the *people's imagination* seemed to be directed to its true destination; it was not bitter or destructive, but creative, "like God's."

It remains for me to express my gratitude to the many people who gave me help, advice and encouragement in making and publishing my translations, in particular to Julie Curtis, Duncan Glen, Felix Philipp Ingold, Jerry Janecek, Jim Kates, Ilya Kutik, Angela Livingstone, Murdo Macdonald, Richard Price, Siân Reynolds, Léon Robel, Jerrold Shiroma, Daniel Weissbort, Antony Wood, and at New Directions, Jeffrey Yang. And as always with love, to Gena and Galya.

Peter France
Edinburgh
July 2002

CHILD-AND-ROSE

VERONICA'S BOOK

MY DAUGHTER'S FIRST SIX MONTHS
JANUARY – JULY 1983

FOREWORD

> *He cannot bear to see a cloud upon her face . . .*
> Dombey and Son

My daughter is in the country just now. As I write, I can hear her distant voice of some time ago (it is nighttime, we are travelling by train, she can't sleep, she is four years old already, and she quietly sings a made-up song to herself: "The moon is my mama, I fly up to the sky, and she feeds me").

And it is strange for me now to be speaking not of her, but "in connection with her." Strange to be switching to "authorship" – and in doing so I gradually attune my voice in the first place to readers in that country which gave to humanity, through the love of Dickens, a whole "daughterly" world.

I always wanted a daughter. "She, the future she" figured even in my most youthful dreams. I think this is partly due to an unconscious revolt against the "cult of the son" in the people among whom I grew up; from childhood on I was repelled by *manfulness* (of the Hemingway type for instance) and attracted by an indeterminately "sacred" *femininity* . . . – perhaps indeed this was how I first became receptive to a kind of "poetry of nature."

My generation grew up without fathers. I need only say that in my village there were 300 households and that more than 200 husbands never came back from the war (some of those who did return became the nucleus of the collective farm and village council mafia – I can personally vouch for this – and their violence and cruelty were directed precisely against this poor *femininity*, which still flickered on like a faintly burning candle in the depths of history).

The coming of a daughter was for me, above all, a renewal of womanliness and femininity in my tribe (and this at a time when

5

my tribal roots – as if they still flamed brightly *somewhere* – were burning ever more intensely within me).

Let me put it still more clearly. The birth of a daughter was for me the *return*, the *resurrection* of my mother. My mother, who died early, still appears to me as a kind of *sacred shining* in the midst of a life which has been all but transformed into a "natural" hell by the dreadful power of the immense Opposite Semblance of the people.

For me the "people" too is simply my mother and her sufferings. And this *other people* of mine (the real people, not its *opposite*) has in the last analysis only persisted in dreams-as-in-snows ("Ever further into the snows" is the title of my most recent book).

One further point: long ago I began wondering why in the world of art there exist *canonic* forms of motherhood, whereas *paternal feeling* in literature generally means no more than the "paternal instinct."

And in my daughter's "Book" I tried to give shape to the principle of *fatherhood* (there are in European literature a few works in which "fatherly" feeling is expressed *post factum*, one of the earliest of them being perhaps the "Laments" of the sixteenth-century Polish poet Jan Kochanowski, poems addressed to the memory of his daughter Ursula).

A small group of poems is included in this English-language edition which were not published in the first edition of the "Book." They are poems about the "period of likenesses." I am convinced (and this is a little "discovery" of mine) that from the first weeks of life up to about the age of three, children *experience*, undergo and bear, both in and upon themselves, moments, days, and weeks of *likeness* and *likenesses* with a multitude of relations, both living and "departed." The little ones (or rather "some forces" within them) seem to be painfully seeking – eventually – finding what are to be their own "permanent" features.

Where people do not respect one another, they may well love children (the "flowers of life," as Gorky put it). But *respect for children*, conscious respect for them, always demands a particular spiritual-religious standard (and I leave this statement without any explanatory notes).

6

It was this awareness that I wanted to express in "Veronica's Book." Somewhere in these pages one can sense my recollection of one of the points in Swedenborg's teaching about man, who is created "incomplete and imperfect" so that in the future he may be "worked on" by That, of Which it is better not to speak (especially in our so rational age).

Observing children of the age of my daughter in her "Book," I am astonished now that I was able to see so much in Veronica's first six months of life. But so it was. And now, when there are already half a dozen translations of the "Book," I once again *thank my daughter for her book, and "my" book* – the happiest in all my "creative" life.

Gennady Aygi
14 July 1989
Moscow

DEDICATION

snows shine white
already grown-up read without me
oh you my ahgagaya
(this word is your second in your house)
with the dark of the head now expands
the dark without minds of our poor Earth
this little book and again
snows shine white

14 November 1983

IN PLACE OF A PREFACE

to my daughter

You do not yet speak in *words*. You express yourself – with your face, your smile, your babble, your "new-born" (as yet unlearned) movements – and this often reminds me of the state of the poet before beginning to write (many know this quietness which "contains something," this kind of "buzz," the still unformed intonation and the special searching power; the gaps in the rhythm and the tense pauses fuller of meaning than any particular "sense") – in a word, you are a creator, not yet "speaking out". . . – and I have tried, as far as possible, to write down from these "unspoken words" something which is prompted essentially by you.

And this book is deliberately devoted to your "wordless" (but as I have said, *creative*) period.

Later we shall talk in words (but that will be something different).

You receive gifts. Love. Toys. My love you already know. "Toys?" By way of toys, I have included in *your* little book some of my *trifles* of long ago.

Sometimes I sing to you (badly). As your paternal grandmothers and grandfathers would have sung to you. Let some of their songs reach you – in a variant by your father (and likewise a version of a Tatar song). I have also included in your book two youthful tales of mine. Could I have imagined then that a quarter of a century later such a daughter would be born to me?

14 July 1983

TWO EPIGRAPHS

Veronica, you are necessary . . .
Leonid Lavrov

. . . And
Veronica's Hair, even here – I plaited,
unplaited,
I plait, unplait,
I plait.
Paul Celan

PROLOGUE:
CHANT – FATHERHOODLAND

If we break this oath, may hops sink
in the Volga and iron float up
(from a treaty between the Bulgars
and the Russians, 985 AD)

if
for you I have passed on
then hops will sink
in-love-like-a-sea
(*ay-iya-yur*)
but when *without me you pass by*
iron will float up
from singing-like-a-sea
(*ay-iya-yur*)

1983–1984
Moscow-Kaunas

ON THE DAY OF FIRST MEETING

could of veneration
this my slowed-down
looking . . . – and what self-recognition
of another world
circles – close by?. . . – not a look – but untouched Word-Face:
oh brief equality: One – it cannot be said! for the same Looks
with the same silence
(One – as the face – at the One)

18 January 1983

MY DAUGHTER'S FIRST WEEK

the quietness
where the child is – seems uneven
within limits – of fragile lightshadows: emptiness! – for the world
    Grows
in her – to Listen
to Itself
in its Fullness

22 January 1983

HEAVEN-GRAMOPHONE

from the fields
continuing out of pain
soon my child
there will be
for you too a schubert:
Always-Unvollendete
somewhere above pain
to be unending
from the fields

February 1983

OR – WHO LOVES TO ME

with what then do I love?
or – who loves to me?
I do not know
for – despite all my *obscenity*
so often
for the baby now
I seem – without changing – sacredly-painfully
(it turns in a circle)
pure

4 March 1983

APPEARANCE IN A SMILE

and a flower opened – to smile on the face:
made new
(so much in solitude)
the *mother-come-again*
shuddered:
oh this circle! turn me so: not to come to my senses or to visions:
praise to Pity
as to God – for this strange-and-only time:
it narrowed – and flashed past!
I know no beginning or end:
only lightwhirl!
(and so strangely including – me)

4 March 1983

ON DAYS OF ILLNESS

1

the baby's illness the trees' disquiet

2

in velvet of flowers I go to sleep tossing and turning
with cheeks tossing and turning
amid floods: like a dream made of clumsy circles:
of belatedly-needless tears:
as if for my mother . . . or for whom then?
clearly – all the more in this mish-mash – clearly:
in any case – not for our Lord

3

and trees were once
like brothers in mist – into their poverty
Came God amid snowdrifts (Continuing
my silence as work:
with sorrow – amid the trees)

4

oh God the child's shudder

11-12 March 1983

BEGINNING OF THE "PERIOD OF LIKENESSES"

and the forces
of the tribe are stirred – and they float
and turn like wind-and-light – carrying over your face
cloud after cloud: all expressions
of vanished faces –

to manifest to confirm – the "definitive"
appearance – your own:

with fire – standing firm in turbulence! –

(is it not with this same heat that – peering – I shudder:

as if – amid some singing? –

pain – came in like the wind)

March 1983

AND: NOT TOUCHING

one should fear
both children's fingers and tender
leaves — of birdcherry:

because:

there is nothing and no-one terrible in the world only God
  (stronger than kindness! and remembering — keep quiet):

and only:

you know — you

22 April 1983

CONTINUATION OF THE "PERIOD OF LIKENESSES"

a passing gleam: a shade? maternal?
from what depths: from unspeaking
time – forgotten treasure? dream and not dream:
light – reaching the face: revelation
of whom then deep down
with the flash of a bond – that perhaps also raises
white and dark of ancient field and wind?
or is it grief – flickering – in the little face
of father-wandering through unknown first-circle
in attempts to find himself again
in the rising storm of the tribe?
you sleep. . . – but it wakes – ever wider ever stronger –   the
    common-shining:
hammered out in pain
where then is it hiding – your
fresh-and-new-found
appearance – among many others?

April 1983

TRANQUILITY OF A VOWEL

a

21 February 1982

NOW

to O.P.

my friend
oh mother-child
the baby's face moves away
to have strength
to come closer shining-quiet
to the circle features
of the loved-and-loving
(many
separately
One)

2 April 1983

AGAIN – A SMILE

it gleams – without age – the soul of humanity: purified – by the heart of a child (by "work" – she too works! – or rather: by work – unknown – on her behalf) – revealed to the light – invisibly – "comprehensible:" oh-what-can-I-say! – to such a source: its name is "it-only-remains unique!" – but what then – just now – is happening? – I look – I forget – I look . . . – forgetting looking

April 1983

QUIETNESS

oh my quiet god
repeating you like a senselikeness
I seem
long since
in a steady calm: cool you flow
without change . . . – only once I glanced round:
the cherries
had already
gone over . . . – the child
prolongs the smile . . . – only such gurgles of yours
including old heart's weakness ever more intimate
(with a certain whisper)
from time to time – barely – show forth
the clarity of the treasure "my quiet god"

April 1983

BED TIME

in my back I feel always
a heaviness "you have gone"
you drop off (and I start to doze
like some kind of sorrowful
"part")

May 1983

URSZULA AND THE WILD ROSE

to the two-year-old
daughter of my friend,
the Lithuanian poet
Sigitas Geda

the wild rose bush
is scarlet and broad – and this
she can almost hear
creasing her little brow:
suddenly – alerted – it seems
a jolt of the heart
surprised her:
it trembles – in the little face
it continues to spread:
the look
like the brief halt
of a little cloud

May 1983

A LOST PAGE
(OR: SNOW IN THE GARDEN)

1

a page on the wind

2

bwol bzilda grad
ei tselestine
bzilda and grad
ohei verty

3

and not to be found

1961

IN THE FOURTH MONTH: ATTEMPTS AT SINGING

the most fragile
is the purest: out of
deep light (plain in presence
rather than naming)
showing forth with clear-simple-shining: this miraculous
painfully innocent (just slightly painfully questioning)
a-a-of-lullaby
(in firstguessing
like firstcreation)

12 May 1983
village of Demidovo, Tver District

SONG FROM THE DAYS OF YOUR FOREFATHERS
(VARIATION ON THE THEME OF A CHUVASH FOLK-SONG)

> *. . . to drink not from a glass, but from a clear spring.*
> Béla Bartók, *Cantata Profana*

I wandered through the field and there was
not a single haycock in it

I went into the village
and there I saw
not a soul

and the girls were sitting
behind washed panes of narrow windows
and knotting the lace
full of eyes

I looked in the window and I saw
they were betrothing my beloved
in a white dress they decked her
placed a wooden cup in her hand

as she stood before the table

 — I wept and I rocked
outside your window
and you were quiet —

like a candle on the sill
of a lofty church

"I see" I said silently
I said silently "farewell"

having no family I understood – "people"
long afterwards
"there was something" I knew

and I kept nothing in my head
weeping with my cheeks
in my hands

1957–1959

AND: AT FIVE MONTHS

by Breast
or by Heel
(oh how humanly
we figure You)
in power – Entering the child
in the face – in miniature – Taking Shape
You Gaze – Seen by us: and I seem in the wind
tremblingly enfolded – scarlet

6 June 1983

LITTLE TATAR SONG

I took a bucket and I went for water
because there was no water at home.
I sat down beside the bucket and wept
because there was no happiness.

And in those days I was hardly
taller than the bucket.

"Mother" I whispered – the clearing fell silent,
"brother" I said – the dream grew quiet.
What I called by name was silence:
the sun, the oaks, the wormwood.

And to my song alone,
outside the village,
I secretly sobbed out – "sister."

1958

TEA ROSE – THE ONLY ONE IN THE NEIGHBORHOOD

in the face
something added – as if by the wind:
seconds of trembling in it
seem the body – of calixity:
in the temples – seems the weight of folds
rounded and gentle: with sorrow

26 June 1983
Chernomorka, Odessa

NOTE – AFTER ROCKING

to J.S.B.

She painfully looks for a *pacifying rhythm* seeks a *near-melody* from
herself and I all unawares *in order to help her* begin to hum a cradle
song of my own invention to that melody whose *outlines* were just
now tormenting her and she goes to sleep I have noticed several
times that her *attempts* at singing to herself and her *fragments* are like
the birth of *something* (like a child's little steps) I would say "for
bach" oh what a heart he must have had the father – with such a
compassionate maternal spirituality – of the lullaby *spheres*

27 June 1983
Chernomorka, Odessa

STORY OF THE LEVEL-CROSSING GATE
AND THE CROSSING KEEPER'S CABIN

A striped old Crossing Gate
was quite sure of being
the Track's one and only suitor.
And boldly thus he spoke:
"My dear Railway Track,
for the last twenty years
I have been bowing to you,
isn't it time you took notice?"
But the Railway Track answered:
"My dear Crossing Gate,
you are only acquainted
with one small part of me,
you don't know all of me.
I have dozens of admirers.
You had better look for someone
who can be seen at a glance."
Only the Crossing Keeper's Cabin
overheard this conversation.
She stood opposite and wept:
"Lord help me, like a fool
I thought it was to me
he was bowing all these years.
Oh why
did I not die
before this day!"

1958

PURER THAN A TEAR

purer than a tear
this dribble: innocent life
shines in it! – joy:
out of purity
of substance
expressed:
oh Lord
to me

June 1983

ROSES OF ETERI AGED THREE

angels

read
your book

and when were the pages opened?

they sink
(and the mind
any moment
will take flight)

oh windlikeness

swoon
(greater than me)
consumed

1983

RECOGNITION OF THE NAME

whirl of feelings perhaps
(like vertigo)
before consciousness
(as before a mirror):
with some power of sight gleams
and disappears
like some imprisoned shade
the shy – with quiet pauses
babble
of something

June 1983

STORY OF HARLEQUIN GROWN OLD

When I strolled down the streets,
chessplayers crowded in my wake
and mentally worked out their moves
on my breeches.

And when I came to the theater,
all the dolls stared at Harlequin,
and carefully concealed the threads
that pulled at their arms and legs.

And when I put my hands behind my back,
they were like white bunches of flowers
lying on a blue carpet,
and the Columbines gasped after me from the balcony
when I went away home.

And when I had worn out my breeches,
the Columbines said that my hands
were like thistles in the open field.
And the dolls all got married.

And now in the deserted castle
I sit on an old sofa with Rex the yard dog,
we drink coffee, curse Siamese cats
and read poems by Yevtushenko.

20 October 1958
Village of Krasnaya Pakhra outside Moscow,
dacha of V.R.

SMILE (MEANING "BELOVED")

and he
(the smile and voice)
is the same — but nearby is noise and movement (chestnut trees
     and roses)
and the loved voice
the face
are now just one among others: nearest tree among trees
(and yet
that tree: is like the continuation
of the babble
the cries
and the little eyes-wa)

25 June 1983
Richelieu Square, Odessa

MOUSE GONE

there she is

18 November 1982

AGAIN: ROCKING YOU

scarlet
roses – touch the eyes
of the baby:
day – be a circle: – oh butterfly:
come in – to mark:
the moment:
with white

June 1983
Odessa

TOPS OF THE BIRCHES – FROM CHILDHOOD AND TILL NOW

as if
still the same:

oh
stillness anew – after
whisper
look
and hearing –

(and I was forgetting this was all my life forgetting the lullaby that was a voice to remember all my life the lullaby as if noiselessly-pristine with spirit opening me from the beginning promising me expansion free without limit) –

oh
stillness anew – (for a long time no-one):

air – in the tops

of the birches

June 1983

AGAIN – SOMETHING FROM THE
"PERIOD OF LIKENESSES"

"oh – you my you"
I whisper-as-I-swing-you
"oh – you the most the most"

not speaking your name! –

and – like a wordless answer – the sleeping child's expression
(the wind – through all the face)
steady even when flickering:

seems as if deep down grows ever stronger in some way a most
      ancient maternal
secret tranquillity:

like a star
softened – by distance

July 1983

AND: SHE SLEEPS (IN A PRAM) BY THE SEA

face – like the quiet
smoothness – of water:

(only sometimes – waves: ripples whose cause
is – let us say – "herself"):

as if in the one – unknown to us – Lullaby:
of the All-World! –

Its concentration – close-drifting

28 June 1983
Odessa: harbor at Chernomorka

SONG OF SOUNDS

o (a Certain Sun)
in *a*-Heaven (also a Certain one)
to *ye-i-oo-y*-Other (Worlds)
and *a-ye-oo*-Others
to trees-*yu* to insects-*ye* to *a*-children

6 July 1983

IN DAYS OF ILLNESS – DREAM IMAGE

bitter
and damp
was the oneness:
the mouth – having touched the rose
and all
this – transformed into a tear
(dimly
as if
a heavy fault
ancient
in memory):
was I – for a moment entirely
forgetting myself in this
in dessicating – daytime – terror

July 1983

WRITTEN IN THE FIELDS

shine my child (I am all around the shining)
from the one light
I persist in request – to the Other
by the wordless – from reverence – circle:
oh that Unnamed One Protect
a little in what you Surround the child with
oh Let me
be

July 1983

CHUVASH SONG FOR A GIRL YOUR AGE

to a little Hungarian girl, Agi Abel

Ay, the game, the turning game! —
and the high point of that turning
is the spreading elm-tree top,
the top of the elm tree shakes,
drops us into fire and water!

and between fire and water
I brewed beer like fire,
gathered guests, as hair is gathered,
made them play like dolls,
then scattered them like chickens:

— Line up, line up, tsip-tsip! —

now scatter!

1983

STILL REMEMBERING THE SAME TEMPLE

Now
as a little girl
as my daughter.
Like the shining
of my tribe – through the face
in the name of all – in a tear
through the ages undimmed
by emotion (as on the holy face)
now in this day of mine
with you
without words – with you.

1983

LONG WALK

day's
Shining
at full height
(Elevation
in the figure
of Air)
in the harsh wounds
(in air)
of roses

July 1983
Chernomorka, Odessa

50

AND: SOMEWHERE A LITTLE BOY IS SLEEPING

to a little Serbian boy of your age,
Mita Badnyarevich

this
unseen fire – guarded
by unseen winds
and the house full of people
is ever more wind – when – in a little understanding
we seem ever closer
to that source of light: the strongest – through most delicate
weakness: oh as if for the earth – among plants – in radiant
    maturation
it expands – in distant hiddenness
its circle (and all this in the house)
this warmth
that is warmer than earth's possibilities
(unseen – wafted in)

1983

VISION: A YOUNG GIRL

to fling up
in lightning the lines
of delicate temples
and to light up
the eyes with such grief "in my life
I shall not see with earthly eyes
the most possibly-Beloved
of Your beauty!"
and to leave a memory of the one without whom
perhaps
it will be
more sad
precisely — in happiness (and the whisper
will come: I wish:
here without order scattered
by movements
friend
to you from yourself)

3 July 1983
Odessa

PHLOXES IN TOWN

as if
in the impersonal thinking of the world
quiet and clear
here — as in the center of a clearing — p u r i t y
                    t r e m b l e s — and we pass by
not disturbing it
even with the imperceptible
breeze of attention

13 July 1983

LULLABY? IT IS YOURS

are you
big or *little?* you
with your whole self – transforming
my heart into a *lullaby* (the days
go by for us
like years) oh more:
you are creating (oh child) with a *lullaby*
my very self: it has gripped me – and the resonance
expands – as if from the kernel
of the utterly familiar! and turns in a circle – from the depths
of little-immense
you

19 July 1983

EX-LIBRIS – FOR YOU – IN VERSE

a divine metronome
phosphorescent
Wild Apple Tree
of Childhood's name

July 1983

SOMETHING – AGAIN ABOUT A BOY
(VERSE FOR A PHOTOGRAPH)

of suffering and pain
of a single kind:
has it happened
in these eyes
the tilt – so clear –

downwards – to the heart? –

as if to mourn
the heart's loneliness –

all – his life

1974–1983

YOUR FIRST SEA WITH ME

1

Moon Submitting to Sea's Concentration Seeking through
Calm Power of Embracing Equalizing by Tranquil Forging

2

dream
like a baby's little steps
in half-darkness
in noise – heard through sleep – as with
a baby's body
for a long time
little steps

3

Sun Possessing Sea Openly with Paternality of Rays of
Chastity Continuing the Embrace Hammering with Magnificence

July 1983
Chernomorka, Odessa

AGAIN – TRYING TO CATCH EXPRESSIONS

can one
discern
in the wind – shades of wind? –

again
into a circle of light
circling (as with some question
perhaps: a little – with light) –

as in whispering almost without breathing
and in terror – before the meaning
of the movement of lips –

afterwards – and unconscious! –

I enter-as-I-stray

June 1983

LITTLE SONG FOR YOU – ABOUT YOUR FATHER

My father was like a white spice-cake
from a Mari folk-song

My father
was like a white spice-cake,
his goodness
shone
white, –

being swallowed
by the air of the day.

And now in that air
there is no-one,
the bedchamber – in winter – becomes an empty field, –

being swallowed
by the dark of the day.

And before dawn I dream
and my father's sleigh in the field
white as a spice-cake,
a spice-cake,
only there is no-one in it,

but over it
shines and floats
the same – white – goodness, –

being swallowed
by my grief.

1983

WRITTEN DOWN WHILE SITTING WITH YOU
ON THE BALCONY

your speech without words! it seems like my intonations: tunes
without words . . . — but what shyness — is yours — in the content
. . . — have I ever achieved such simplicity of radiance — of enchant-
ment-with-everything! — with a modesty — that seems to gleam! . . .
— with the idea itself . . . — of innocence

12 July 1983

PAUSE IN MY DAUGHTER'S "BOOK"

suddenly
(you are sleeping now
but I see
a look)
I must grieve and abide alone:

as if — all dried up! —

:

I lived on and off (broken branch of needlessness
in one thing then another!
at times needful a little in something
but then
nothing
to anyone —

and at times I shuddered — I shrank with compassion:

in the steady
long-familiar
stillness!) —

:

and you were purest
tear
in the world:
(oh at times to speak with such a tear . . .) —

you were – as in silence
the place – of answer
simple – in simplicity of goodness! . . –

:

and I
(as if in the world
a being
without substance
so strangely
alone) –

longed – to commune in you as in a tear

with your purity

July 1983

OFTEN FIVE-YEAR-OLD ASYA COMES TO SEE US

in thin little Asya
there is overflowing
goodness! and her face knows no limits:
like a noisily-glittering street
over a gully — with a skip-and-a-leap
onward — to shine! and the shining little girl
comes — into our world (yours and mine)
with a smile — still more — outlining
as a guest! . . . and her hands are like a peasant girl's
covered in cuts and scratches "mommy
lets me peel the cucumbers"
and in the company of these delicate-"working" cuts and scrapes
you and I are as if in the circle
of ancient — poor-most-generous childhood
(encompassing
the infinite world)

July 1983

FIELD DREAM

The Bobolink — the Sea
Emily Dickinson

oh lightest
of winds — from the little
star-face
just perceptible over the frock —

it opens wide for me a special field: to live and have our being
with that trueness only! . . . . . the sun
sinks . . . and there among swifts over daisies
is my Bobolink! . . . — on love this sweetest of wounds
is all — your purity:

breath — of the world

July 1983
Moscow, field near Orekhovo-Borisovo

CONTINUATION

I must
plunge deeper
into that shining
(not remembering what you are)
and the understanding
shines shines – and this is for another
I – to understand (continuing the shining
in a new forgetting
to others)

1983

PLAYING FINGER GAMES

> *And the little finger said:*
> *"But I'll run away without saying anything!"*
> from the words of a children's finger game

A call, – oh what sudden – with pain – concentration of music –
fathomless and higher than any possible "height": sounds – pre-
words! . . . – smile, little teeth – fresher than petals: in whiteness! –
tiny nail, questioning look: the world is like a silent question in
reply! – again tiny nail, tear, this thin lock of hair on the neck, and
the finger: to be entrusted – as a charm – to an angel only – and even
then: only in reflection! – babble and nail! . . . – yes, all this is
equality: before the one measure – veneration.

13 July 1983

AND: OATS IN FLOWER BEYOND THE MEADOW

Finishing this book, to you
— out of my childhood

oh dream
the soul is that dream
she is always there in scratches:
the common dream
passes over into a feast-day
and the distance that remains (singing without people)
through and through
rustling
ever more into the distance
is flowering

July 1983

SINGING AND SILENCE

and the little girl-flute sings
when the silence
in the dull-calm city is pure and free
like some field – and also like an echo: brief and fragile
sphere (already she rang out glassily)
in pure concentration
seeming
like a child of god

1983

AGAIN – THE THIRD GRASSHOPPER (NOW – FOR YOU)

with squeak-and-leap! – sketch after sketch
(drawing – on air) –

with a winglet – he rubs out
with a noselet – puts in shadows

and a wash – of radiance-clearing! signs
with sunbeam-chirrup:

– *here* for me
just a flicker – *everywhere!* –

with his legs? both up and down!
his canvas – just one thing:

the sky – not ever drying! –

he's simply (let me tell you) – old father:

Cha-gall!

July 1983

TO A FRIEND – INSTEAD OF A LETTER

to M.F.

and yet
Friend
when
everything falsely-adult-clearsighted has long
been gathering – in a blind fog
out of the darkness cutting – as if building a world
that is always the same separate-and-from-nowhere
they gaze – flowers and children
(and what besides? – in the depths of hushed pre-vision
ever more ancient and distant
are the cries
the reminders
of the birds)

31 May 1984
Moscow, in the metro

FIRST WORDS

Just half-a-dozen of them: like pebbles in the palm . . . – taking care
– not to drop them – and the awkward inspection – with a kind of
shyness: as if – saying slowly: "there . . ." – even a request and a call
are modest gifts: of the whole being.

1983

AGAIN – CLOSENESS OF ROSES

in waves – of movement
of evening light –

peaceful – their childhood . . . –

in glimmering shade – fusing – with you:

flowering-as-sleeping . . . –

(or rather – *abiding*):

now here now there. . . –

(quiet – ever quieter)

July 1983

VISION: A GIRL

not from me
from another
calling forth – a masterpiece of Poetry
passed through the city
Immortality – and now her contemporaneity
is no more – and the Word
fuses with the Sun
and with souls
in another world – and through it all
gleams
like a gift
her young walk! . . . . . – in an unknown principle
is the best – of her now finished
shining – and of the long
(like fires
burning)
fathers

1983

AGAIN – SHE SLEEPS

again
disturbing with special
quietness
(as if of the spirit) . . . . . . and dear to me
like a wound . . . . . . I bend down . . . . . . and she glows
with a criss-crossing
of Bending – as of the Mother . . . . . . breathing threefoldness
of pain . . . . . . that aerial Bending
faintly
touching me
with its radiance

July 1983

ABOUT THIS

whether little or much
the gift – of love
will later come to seem
such emptiness it will have to be filled
with great pain: perhaps you will not see it yourself –

(others will see it) –

as with plenitude – achieved by you
it will start to circle! – the oneness
of the silent friend's former gift
and of sorrowful memory:

a modest (like a spot when eyes are closed)
simple human star –

for the world (or perhaps – just for sky and air)

7 July 1984
Dovainonis, Lithuania
(raspberry canes in the forest)

SOMETHING PRECIOUS

Suddenly: a glance through the window – and I see just this:
your little hand – among flowers

July 1983

AND: THE FIRST HALF YEAR

you are a *peasant baby* out of Rembrandt
these little feet made to walk on plank floors
to fall (mother cannot see everything)
and the knees are bent – obedient to a simple song (to jump and
    skip – more than to be grateful! to help and to sympathize)
the little hands – as if taking bread
(even so – *love* is embraced)
and the kitten-rival "put in its place" by your growing up
in front of the bowl sits quiet
and the Protector? in this picture
he is always in half darkness
with the work (for child and God) of his hands

14 July 1983

CHILD-AND-ROSE

weight
of the child
(*and there – beyond the gate – the one*
shaken by wind
above
the lake)
the weight
of a rosebud
(*in the room next door – the one*
lightly
treading
through the field)

7 July 1984
Dovainonis

EPILOGUE:
LULLABY-SUWALKIE

it has set
(*kupolya kupoleli*):

the sweet sun — *lelyumay:*

alelyum kaleda! —

(quietly: here comes into
the singing — *Demyadis*:

the Tree of God) —

kupolya kupoleli! —

she sleeps — in her cot
my daughter — *lelyumay! —*

alelyum kaleda

14 July 1984
Suwalkie, Southern Lithuania

AND: FAREWELL TO THE BOOK

a

September 1983 – July 1984

A LAST WORD FROM THE AUTHOR

My daughter Veronica (my sixth child) was born on January 14, 1983. The poems in this little book were written for the most part during my hours of direct contact with my daughter: when I was taking her for walks, rocking her in the pram and so on. Hence the "miniature" quality of several of the poems and the "notational" or observational form of some of them.

21 August 1983

SLEEP-AND-POETRY

(NOTES)

1

December – and whenever we are awake – by day or by night – there is always the darkness of December out of the window.

Life is the enduring of this darkness.

Such darkness expands space, as if including it in itself – and it is itself infinite. It is more than city and night – you are surrounded by some single limitless Foul-Weather-Land.

You must endure a few more hours of solitary work. You are one of the *sentinels of night* – "someone must stay awake, someone must be a sentinel," says Kafka.

But you remember the possibility of Refuge, of Salvation even, from the anguish inspired by the Foul-Weather-Land.

And at last you pull the blanket over your head and wrap the other end of it under your feet. And then you wait for *Sleep* to envelop you on all sides. To fold you into its Lap. You hardly think about what this resembles . . . Some kind of return? To what? To where?

2

A huge headline in *Literaturnaya Gazeta*: "The riddle of Morpheus solved?"

Perhaps we shall soon be reading: "The riddle of waking solved?"

Why is a person composed of waking only, why is he or she nothing but waking, and sleep not merely the person, but something else, something "other"?

Why are we like strangers to ourselves when we have "business" with sleep?

Clearly we cannot forgive *sleep* the oblivion, the "loss" of our "I" – the very thing that at the same time we so thirst after.

It is as if we were "playing at Death" with it, without knowing the essential thing about death, just as children play at war, knowing nothing of *murder*.

3

But remember, before the inward sleep merges with the outer – with Foul-Weather-Sleep, – before you become – remembering and not-remembering yourself – existent and as if "not-born" – remember "those who are on the march."

And remember, shuddering, Nerval: in the freezing cold, the empty street . . . , – Nerval knocking at the flophouse door. Not recalling, not remembering – his mother . . .

4

Sleep-Haven. Sleep-Escape-from-Waking.

5

Speaking of the links between Poet and Public, Poet and Reader, we shall consider here only the most recent times, and specific places.

And using the subject before us, let us ask ourselves where, in which literature, there is most *sleep*.

There is a great deal of it in "non-committed" poetry.

6

Waking is so much "everything" that it has not been given a separate God, as *sleep* has.

But in any case aren't we talking of different ways of looking at one and the same boundless Sea – the conceivably-and-boundlessly Existing.

7

There are periods — extremely brief ones — when the *truth of the poet* and the *truth of the public* coincide. They are the times of poetry's public action. The audience experiences the same thing that the poet proclaims from the platform or stage. And then we hear a Mayakovsky.

Public truth is the truth of action. The audience wants actions, the poet calls to action. Is there any room here for *sleep*? There is no *sleep* in the poetry of the Futurists (only dreams, mostly ominous ones).

8

Sleep-Love-of-Self.

"Sinless" sleep, it seems, is possible on a desert island. However, we know that Robinson Crusoe on his island soon found for himself obligations to other *living creatures*. And let us not forget his prayers to the Creator.

9

Poetry has no *ebb* and *flow*. It *is*, it *abides*. Even if you take away its "social" efficacy, you cannot take away its living, human fullness, profundity, autonomy. After all, it can visibly penetrate also into those spheres where *sleep* is so active. To "dare" to dwell in *sleep*, to draw nourishment from *it*, to communicate with *it*, such, if you like, is the unhurried confidence of poetry in itself — it does not need to be "shown the way," to be "authorized," to be controlled (so too, correspondingly, the reader).

Does poetry lose something in such circumstances, or does it gain? Let me leave this as an unanswered question. The main thing is that it *survives*. Drive it out of the door, it comes back through the window.

10

Waking up is a thousand-fold "new birth."

And yet, where does this *regret for something* on waking come from?

Perhaps we are grieving unconsciously for the "material" of life, which has been consumed, unbeknown to us, during the night – and for the thousandth time – on the dark, wordless bonfire of Sleep?

And so the truth of poetry gradually disappears from public places – it retreats into the separate lives of separate individuals.

The reader changes, – now he is not occupied with faceless "common affairs," now he experiences his life in the light of the problematic phenomenon of Existence. This must not be thought of as his own selfish "affair" – his experience of existence can be *exemplary*, can show the way – a model of human life. This reader needs a poet who speaks *only for him, only with him*. The poet in such a case is the only companion he can trust.

The "shape" of the connection between poet and reader is changing. Now it is not from *stage* to *auditorium*, to the *ear*, but from *paper* (often not even from print) to *person*, to the *eye*. The reader is not *led*, not *summoned*; he is *conversed with* as an equal.

12

The general state of sleep, its "non-visual" atmosphere, is sometimes more important and leaves a greater impression than the dream itself. (As if the atmosphere of a cinema were to affect us more than the film).

I shall never forget an uncomplicated dream I had some twenty years ago: the sun is setting; in a kitchen garden, just above ground level, the leaves of a sunflower are gleaming. I have rarely felt such emotion, such happiness as then, on "seeing" this dream.

I need no "Freudian interpretations" here. I simply don't want any ("leave me in peace").

"Symbols?" – You can discover them easily enough.

But you cannot include in the luminous circle of this dream-sleep the most important *factors* (you can only *take account* of them, but you cannot *experience* them, for they belong to someone else): I was sleeping in my native porch, in my native village (and beyond stretched, like a Sea of Happiness, the boundless Field!), my mother was somewhere close by (perhaps in the same kitchen garden . . . perhaps her sleeves were damp from brushing the *hem* of the Guardian-Forest), there was such a triumphant "presence of all and of each!"* – and the *absent* was still hiding – as from daylight – like a thief in the forest . . .

Sleep-World. Sleep-maybe-Universe . . . Not only with its Milky Way, but with a little star too on the outskirts of your village, a star which is perhaps visible to the vision-soul.

13

I hope it won't seem as if I consider an increased "incidence" of sleep the main characteristic of the type of poetry I am speaking of. It has many other aims and many other "materials" – that is why it is "non-committed" (we shouldn't expect it to "commit" itself to *sleep* after all!).

But since we are talking about *sleep*, then let us say that the connections of this kind of poetry with the Reader are so intimate that they can *share sleep* one with another.

14

Sleep-Poetry. Sleep-Conversation-with-oneself. Sleep-Trust-in-one's-Neighbor.

*An expression from the author's poems.

15

But what about poetry's heroic qualities, its active life, its civic responsibility?

We must not forget indeed that somewhere at the same time and in the same country Mandelstam — who is needed only by a dozen readers — is actively meeting his death. He has nothing to do with *sleep*. As another poet put it, he knows only a "great *insomnia*."

16

Sleep-Lethe.

Leonid Andreyev describes the risen Lazarus: he has learned something in Death, he remembers something, something which cannot be defined in human language.

Perhaps he learned *nothing*?

(How bold we can be in our "knowledge" of Death).

A friend, regaining consciousness after a deep swoon, says: "There was nothing, there was not even any 'there,' I was, and then . . . — what can I say? . . — and now — once again — I am."

There are states of sleep like that swoon.

Sleep which is often, with "poetic imprecision," compared to death.

17

When public truth is impossible, the *poet-as-tribune* is replaced by the *platform poet*. The connection between such a poet and the public is like a mutual agreement to "play at truth" ("we know the truth, — we have left it at home, — that is not why we have gathered here — why talk about unpleasant things, better enjoy ourselves").

What place is there here for *sleep*, with its anxieties, its complicated, tragic *Individuality* (for a person's *sleep* is perhaps his Individuality — expanded — both self-trusting and searching, confessing, demanding?).

18

And even so, the comparison of Sleep with Death (a very frequent, almost universal one) is conventional and approximate. In such cases, it is not as if we knew something about Death-in-Itself (as if we knew what It contained)? We know Its traces, we know our fear of It. Comparing Sleep with Death, we are most probably speaking only of this fear.

Schopenhauer astonishes me when he gives such a categorical definition of sleep as time "borrowed from Death."

19

Who were the poets of whom Mayakovsky exclaimed: "I'm fed up" at the start of his most active career? Annensky, Tyutchev, Fet. The very poets in whose poetry there is the most *sleep* in all of Russian literature.

There is no *sleep* in Mayakovsky (only dreams, invented, "constructive"), there is a great deal of it in Pasternak.

But at the same time let us give thanks to Sleep (I want to say to Mother-Sleep — it is strange that its gender is masculine in both Russian and French — it must be the God-Sleep), thanks that it is not only a hiding place, a sleeping bag — an imitation of the mother's lap — thanks that the surge of its waves also bakes something for the hearing we know as "poetic," — "bakes likes waffles"* — remembered in the blood — sound-clusters of darkness, — disposing them — between pauses of emptiness — like shadow-boundaries — of non-paper spaces! — which can, however, also define "poetic spaces;" thanks — for its light-clusters gleaming, perhaps, like faces — still unknown (oh every night — in sleep — these light-images — with shadow-hieroglyphs!) . . .

*A quotation from Pasternak's *Second Birth*.

Indistinct, "sea-like" labor of sleep! — we believe in it as a lover believes in the life-giving influence of his beloved.

But — "practically" — how often we turn to Sleep (not intending to, and thus giving ourselves entirely) for "artistic" help. A life of conscious thought will not take us to those reminiscences, those depths of memory which *sleep* can display in a moment of illumination. The "Phonotèque" and "Phototèque" of the Empire of Sleep are, by the grace of Sleep, always at our disposal, and they contain "photographs" and "recordings" of the most complex feelings, the most ancient — and thus the freshest — and most subtle of observations.

Let me repeat here the confession I once made to a friend: "It may seem funny, but I have to say that I write my best things on the very brink of sleep."

Of course, this is a special kind of sleep . . .

The poet would gladly agree to things being arranged so that he could do without food. Indeed, it would be better for him. But do not deprive him of *sleep*, Lord . . .

21

"I trust people who get up early," admits a young woman.

There are poets who do not concern themselves with the material of *sleep*. There are those who are often concerned with it, but they are fighters against sleep, *sleepfighters*. René Char. Mandelstam is without doubt an "early riser."

22

Sleep-Whisper. Sleep-Roar.

Man is rhythm.

Sleep must in all ways "permit" this rhythm to be itself (not to be diminished or interrupted by the influence of other rhythms).

Sleep-Poem-in-its-own-right.

23

You could put it this way: a human being is his or her *sleep*, the character of the sleep contains the character of the person.

Dostoevsky's *sleep*: "I sleep and wake as many as ten times in one night, every hour or less, often sweating."

It is like a film which breaks in an almost methodical way when it is projected. Similarly, in Dostoevsky's novels (and particularly their concluding sections) a series of chapters one after another finish with an explosion of events.

24

As a person takes decisions in relation to life and death, so he manifests his will in relation to *sleep*.

Sleep, which is given us for *rest*, can be transformed into a means of *self-forgetting*.

Sleep-Love-of-Self.

To experience oneself. To delight in visions, in *sleep*. For consolation and joy one's own self is enough. A person experiences his own feelings, his flesh, almost his "own atoms."

How this resembles the love of intoxication. (In the same way, how a so-called "drunken delirium" resembles dreams).

A subject for a thesis: "Sleep in the literature of southern and northern countries." In which is it more present?

Northern darkness envelops man like the indistinct material of *sleep*.

Sleep exists at both poles of the opposition "Happiness-Unhappiness."

Reduce these notions to the antithesis "Joy-Grief" and *sleep* disappears.

Sleep likes to inhabit broad notions. We find it in "war," but not in "battle."

27

"I belong to the gods," said Velemir Khlebnikov in his poem "For ten years the Russians threw stones at me," a kind of last will and testament.

And his *sleep* is the sleep of Blessedness. The *sleep of the holy sinner* (undirected bleessedness of sleep).

> *Sene, son of sky,*
> *Sow somnolent sable and strength*
> *On settlement and soil.*
> *Chary of day, with a chalice*
> *Of blue wine charm*
> *Me, earthdweller, with the wave*
> *Of one foot breaking*
> *After another.*

This is such a "lyre-like voice" that it seems as if Pushkin would have gasped in quiet rapture at these lines.

Khlebnikov the futurian, unlike the other Russian futurists, belongs to the "sleepers," the dreamers. But he is vigilant too, like a tempted saint. Later in the same poem we read:

> *My steps,*
> *Mortal steps, are sequence of will.*
> *My mortal locks I bathe*
> *In the blue vapor of your quiet*
> *Waterfall and suddenly shout*
> *And break spells; the surface formed*
> *By a straight line which joins*

In 317 days earth and sun
Is equal to a rectangle's surface
One side of which is the earth's
Diameter, the other the road
Light treads in one year. And you rise
In my reason, holy figure
of 317, among clouds
Which do not believe.

Will shakes off *Sleep*. And the mathematical calculations of time begin (they take up the second half of the poem, I have cited only a small part of it).

28

Sleep-Light . . . Sleep-Illumination.

Whence this sudden Sea of Light? Perhaps it is a "cyclical" return of the causeless Unhoped-for Joy?*

Sleep-Healing.

29

The dream of Petya Rostov before his death is not just a dream, so powerfully and fundamentally is it directed by the young man's musical gift. Here, at the second level of this dream, we have: Sleep-the-creator, Sleep-the-artist, man-the-artist. Expanded plenitude of the human being (everything in him is "switched on," the sleep-artist, the sleep-man too has "begun to speak"). And perhaps – as if something were "switched off" – the waking-man, who a moment before was busy – with battle (not the fullness of War!) – is really a "narrow man."

*The name of a famous icon used in Blok's poetry.

30

Even if we have got up in good time, and haven't even taken half an hour's sleep at the expense of our nearest and dearest, even so, "on waking we feel somehow guilty, as if we had behaved badly towards someone," as a friend of mine said recently.

Were we too freely, too "unreservedly" occupied with ourselves in sleep? Did we allow ourselves "everything?"

Clearly there is a kind of sleep where conscience does indeed "doze off."

There is no *sleep* in my *rose-poems*. They are the opposite of *sleep-poems*. Waking, beloved waking (I have written of "dangerous waking, containing the loved ones") is the incandescence of roses flowering.

Look at a person whom not long before you disliked, who perhaps even provoked hostile feelings in you, look at him as he sleeps.

For some reason you will feel pity for him. Pity for his sleeves that stick out, for his hands . . . Pity for his clothes, for some reason. (Awake, his costume resembled "worldly," "institutional," even "family" armor).

He is all trust in Something, in Somebody. And naturally in Someone, who is immeasurably greater than you, the observer.

But even so, there is here also a trust *in You*.

33

Insomnia. No-Sleep. Antipodes of Sleep, ominous, hostile to us. Sleep's double defined by a "No." For it is not just that we "cannot sleep." And it is more than Pseudo-Sleep. It is as if for hours on end we are penetrated by disintegration of "No" atoms. Not death, but a demonstration of destruction, a display of the "means" by which our gradual, "natural" end is prepared.

34

Let us imagine now the watchful sleep of a hunted man, who in his sleep expects to be attacked, caught, beaten. His face is like a screen, and he will awake if even a feeble shadow falls on this screen.

Transparent, translucent face. And through this partition seems to peer – the soul.

35

Sleep is the cultivator of our fears. It intensifies them, weakening our resistence to them.

36

But where do we not see this face-screen, this transparent *partition*?

There is the repulsive sleep (if you have had occasion to see it) of *thugs*. The same sleeves, parts of the body and clothing which in the previous case made you feel pity, do not now seem abandoned to the power of God's will, but remain real, "belonging to the day," "ready for living," *looking at you* in the familiar everyday way; all this collection of corners of clothing and projections of the body is indeed only *resting*.

37

Oh, Sleep-Ablution! How can we deserve to be visited by you? Wash away, carry off these images – the raw material of nightmares!

38

In poems about *insomnia* the word "conscience" is constantly recurring. No-Sleep (not just the "absence of sleep") penetrates to the pivot of a man.

And the most *"conscience-bound"* of Russian poets, the one who more than anyone works with *conscience*, Innokenty Annensky, is the greatest martyr to Insomnia in the whole of world poetry.

His "Old Estonian Women" is a poem close to shouting about insomnia and it is subtitled "Fragments of a nightmarish conscience."

Annensky's *sleep-poems* are also agonizing; they do not descend into sleep, but leave the sphere of sleep for sorrow, for the cold dawn of searching, tormenting self-consciousness.

39

And now, suddenly waking in the darkness, not yet having had time to get your thoughts together enough to begin again to *love yourself with them*, you will suddenly feel that a certain "you" is a strange, heterogeneous, and because of the impossibility of experiencing certain emptinesses, a partly-*unlawful* place;

you will suddenly realize that you are not so completely and utterly "I," self-consciousness, — suddenly, like something empty, you will uncover in yourself — in "topographically"-undefined gaps — both "regions" of dust and ashes, and regions of such lifeless "materiality," such as is built (as if on a building site!), and seems made for spades, for the hammer, for the windy street;

(and now, for some reason you find yourself in a corridor, and what if that is all there is, what if from here you will *never* return *to anything*; — and you will be — unexpectedly — *so abolished* — nothing but "not," and soon thought too will be extinguished and only the *corridor* will remain; — and those sleeping beside you? — *who* represented to them conversation, presence, existence, — will remains like that — afterwards — at table — opening wide — their mouths — with astonishment? . .), —

such, in the intervals of sleep, are you, suddenly finding yourself in a corridor, as if in a remote corner of some deserted, universal Mistiness.

40

And even so, "let us plunge into the night."*

There are people there. There, in the depths of sleep, is the communion of the living and the dead.

And just as we do not picture the souls of the dead as "social" or "national," so, if only in sleep, let us be trustful in the souls of the living, — and for this let us wish ourselves clear sleep, *sleep* which seems to have forgiven us.

For who besides Poetry would allow himself to do this? . . .

Moscow, 20–24 January 1975

---

*Quotation from Kafka.

BEFORE AND AFTER
THE BOOK

ROSES IN TOWN

to R.B.

oh this color of their wounds: above them: reflected!

there is their suffering. . .
in town — as in the field
freely-evident
like openness of souls

its connection with the eye is easy
when the face — as by pain
is corroded — by vision

and clearly arises
the common changing of two pains:

and purely — com-passion . . . —

oh pain — from pain that is without:
our second reality! . . . —

reddening cloud
in the world's sad slumber

(but the unquiet gleams! . . .

as *is said by them*
of you and of me! —

thus we ourselves could not)

1972

MOZART: "CASSATION I"

to S. Gubaydulina

mozart godlike mozart straw compasses godlike

blade wind paper infarct madonna wind jasmine

operation wind godlike mozart cassation twig jasmine

operation angel godlike rose straw heart cassation mozart

1977

NOW THERE ARE ALWAYS SNOWS

like snow the Lord that is
and is what is the snows
when the soul is what is

the snows the soul the light
and all is only this
that those like death that is
that like them too it is

confess that it is so
among light darkness is
when once again the snows
Oh-God-Again-The-Snows
how can it be it is

and is not to be checked
as corpses are and not

oh Deathmask-Land that is
no question that it is
then when the People verb
which signifies is not

and that such being is
what is this doing here
the Face is such a Mask
it seems there only is
the land Darkness-and-Face

the Epoch-such-a-corpse

and one there is that is
when straightway they are not
– oh God again the snows! –
they are not one thing is
only the Deathness-Land

it is as is and not
and only by this is
but is what only is

miracle sudden swirl
there is no Deadness-Land
oh God again the snows
the soul the snows the light

Oh God again the snows

but be there there are none
the snows my friend the snows
the soul the light the snow

oh God again the snows

and snow that is there is

1978

ABOUT THIS

This
is not Argument.
And if I name it,
it is simple indication:
"Here – is Perfection."
(Place of Suggestion.
In This it is Present.
I remain silent.)
"God?"
A quotation: from God.

1980

SNOW – IN AN "OLD" DISTRICT OF MOSCOW

and snow (and ever more
meager)
like soot again: once more the smearedness
of corners of the alley of pillars and shut-up stalls
of sparse – seen from windows – tree-trunks
with damply-peaceful dimness (like beds in the dark of gardens)
of half-snowdrifts
and half-"something"-people (and this sympathy
now – with slowing of human-seeming time
ever more and more nearly
warm)

1982

AMONG OAKS

the sky is quiet – and here
burn –

foundations – of fathers –

preserving the house and the land
clearly and freely – in clear disquiet! –

eyes that once god-gazed
see –

created – from each – without exception – a world

of depth (simply – like life) –

of blazes – of brotherhoods

13 June 1984
Dovainonis, Lithuania
at Vladas Didžokas' house

LEAF-FALL AND SILENCE

1

so that I
in myself should pray,
You
are not filled for me – with prayer,
and in evident powerful
absence
I am ringed, encircled.

2

But in her
the child – I cannot
pray. She is in herself
a prayer. You, in this quiet circle
Yourself
are utterly
in Yourself.

3

What am I
in the Silence – as in steady Light?
Or in fire. But the sick trees' frozen equality is living. And You,
        next to this –
are clarity, – oh, impenetrable clarity. Compared to it
death is a promise . . . – is something other! . . . And in a dead
        circle
unendurably
falls from a tree – a leaf.

1984

AGAIN: APPEARANCE OF A BLUETIT

to E. Epshtein

this blackish-green
cloud of innocent power
I more than once roused beneath heaven –

again as in far-off years
it shrank to this bird – to the trusting-shy trembling
of a flower – brought in by the wind and the snow:

widening grief
into house and edge of the city –

the flowering a tap on the window:

in the noise of friends' arrival surviving
a minute or two –

(I listened to their speaking
as if
I were sleeping more brightly more gladly)

1985

SNOW AT MIDDAY

to my daughter – on her third birthday

"I see I love" – and it is light so light
and "I remember I love it outside the window unseen"
then – it is touchingly-dim! – from the ever more common
lighttreasure! – and human joy somewhere there quivers
all – made new
by quiet sympathy: addition of your movements-emotions –

from a life that is trusting-clear

1986

AND – STRANGELY: "SOMEWHERE" – MY DAUGHTER

*Once in a field, – long ago, – she – suddenly began speaking
to me in a whisper. These continuing – and already two-sided
conversations we called – "our secret."*

mine simply to struggle – to fail – to be torn
by a single misfortune – like a shudder of death! –

and to flare up – to droop: to rise up again –

in mindlessness-mind:

"oh my daughter – my bride – oh baby:

rustling – of child-mother . . ." –

not dividing them – to burst into tears! –

(and a far-off "daddy" – as if nearby: thunder)

1986

TWO LITTLE SONGS FOR THE TWO OF US

1

what – now – is consolation? –

song's meagerness – heart's contraction
and "not-hereness" and goodfornothingness! –

in this frozen destitution
of branches – steadfastly indifferent
gypsy-like going to sleep –

poverty – in the wind

2

we are among those who are poorer than poor
no more than just barely
with Church Mice in their element
long Swept by Misfortune

1986–1987

AGAIN: AIR IN THE TOPS – OF BIRCHES

lighter:

:

freedom:

:

(of old)

1987

MY DAUGHTER'S AUTUMN WALK

suddenly — a strange wind
seemed
to float obliquely
through the inner — roar of ruin:

lightly liberating . . . —

— oh thus — to be abolished! and prolong
transfigured — our being in the world:

in the futile shape steadfastly-transparent
of soot-raiment of those who were scattered-and-trampled
in ravines
above ravines:

in the gleaming of golden day . . . —

and again *that same roar* — but newly transformed
in distant melody burning
single-singular-deep:

"little girl in the street
won't you press your lips to my hands" —

but myself in an alien echo
I forgot how it started! — and in twilight's meager moisture
I smear myself as in liquid
made of ash and of cinder of humiliated love —

(shuddering palm of the hand — "a person"):

and evening spreads and glimmers – in the hand burns the circle
of the flaming trace of childhood! –

what – life-a-suburb in all things? no less
dull – in vacuity – the somewhere-world:

and for me – one alien-expelled
the self has long been enough
to become singly-dead desolation –

and in a concealed-final hearth
inwardly I crumble: in sooty-growing-quiet! –

and yet – *while stifling in this* – suddenly:

in a wound-gaze I surface: for a child

1987

NOW SUCH A ONE ALSO

you – image of calm that is indeed whole
with no dimly-dangerous somewhere beyond this calmness
and free – barely-orphaned
Russia-river . . . – and then – little by little – the gleaming in you
of another fair one – what we call primal beauty and perfection
and to say again beauty and whisper it is fitting! – oh pure with
    long abandonment
ever more quiet: as if in unending toil! – long ago this was – and
    already we cannot remember
as if above many souls
somewhere in the land – after us – continuing to grow quiet
something of heaven-river

1987
village of Denisova Gorka,
Tver district

HOUSE – IN THE GROVE OF THE WORLD

dedicated to little Alexandra

house – or world
where I went down to the cellar
a white day it was – and I
was going to get milk – a long time it lasted
going down with me: it was
day – like a river: of brimming
expansion of light
leaping into the world: I
was the creator of an event
in the age
of firstcreations –

to the cellar – long ago – it was simple longlasting –

the grove white in the mist
and this
child with a pitcher – eyes a universe – and heaven
sang in all its breadth – like a special song
spread over the world
by women – simply shining in the movement
of its whiteness – into the expansion of the field
where in voice I was beginning –

to be – a universe-child:
I was – for it sang and it was

1987

THIS AUGUST'S PHLOXES

now – I cannot get warm: slowing
with their calmness – my steps! . . . –

– and the wor-rk of mo-ur-ning went on
(long ago – in their featherlight world. . .) –

and what – more detailed – can I tell you? –

but that – you yourself – invaded – with a distant cry:

. . . with that storm unseen I shall stay . . . –

until when? – . . . you run stretching out hands:

oh whiteness! . . . oh dissolve – into yourself! –

(separate the tears on the face)

3 August 1987
Wood at Lembolovo

SUPPER: HOUSE OUTSIDE TOWN

to M. Geller

1

even the sugar is murmuring: "and do you remember how they came
for you — how they came at dawn" — although now the disaster is
another — and the thought now is not of that

2

someone was saying "I" someone whispered "bread": "this is sleep-
and-family" — clashed fleetingly in far-off singing: I leant-and-stiff-
ened — as if rising somewhere like a burning pillar amid others in an
ancient festive-field: to cast myself out from the chorus of those who
move . . . —

— and later a line was traced — in blood! —

and then I saw — from another hidden chorus: of people-suffering —
from forgotten depths flaring up in the brain — and perhaps in the
memory of body-as-soil: to forget in secret — I saw children (and
with dawn was mingled "I-am-sleep-and-family": like singing —
with light! — with a wound in the temples — like a mouth)

3

"how then you walked" — this quiet thing keeps on murmuring —
"how then you walked through the grove"

1988

GIFT – A BIRCH GROVE

to my daughter

but my friend but child-friend
that the soul can grow heavy
in a manner never yet known
your father-friend had to learn –

"be turned to stone?" – for me
there was no such liberation:

in allfilling sensitive allfirmness
within me you were my child
so much not leaving me yourself –

and in feeling-vision becoming such
(in one – steadfast – and somehow steady – torment)
I wandered – not seeing the world: and saw – only you:

was it squeezed like that – in slow patience
comprehensible – of itself – the fusion? –

then – as a gift to you – I remembered only
the peripheral dearly-bright sobering
(spark-like – burning in itself – in covert-wild eternity)
immortal-strong grove of birches –

when the world's chastity
rang – with their fearful – hardening – whiteness

1988

AWAITING A FRIEND

to Wolfgang Kasack

brothers in the kitchen at night nothing but things in the kitchen
such — as we know when not seeing our near ones:
oh long calm — this is poverty seemingly no-one's in the being
    on earth
of barely-for-something utensils . . . — so leaving to us a joy so replete
    with trifles
as in a clearing among long-ago trees
as if barely-self-surpassing-upheld a light shining
with warm close pre-speaking:
 — brothers in the kitchen kindly life

1989

HOUSE IN THE FIELD

all very simple: a mouse — rubbish quivering
and wind round the corner
and there — a road in the rain at night
and just here — in the garden — a table
abandoned: and the talk — all sidelong and aslant
clinging and rustling
of familiar (like an old jersey) leaves
and homeland-mist — ever more ever nearer
with the soul-glance — of long gone long gone
(how can I speak it) mother . . . —

 — here the bell of the Tyrol sings out
itself alone: riv-ver: all wide open
like purest blood. . . . . —

swallow in hiding and mouse
call out to the heart: you shut the door
and with twilight of soul in the house
feeling your way . . . — so the world is ended:

closed up — with a long forgotten whisper

1990

TOGETHER

again this refugee woman with children in the corridor – hardly room
    to lie on the floor – over faces again go the circles
of policeman's lamps – and the next person's back is neither kind nor
    unkind – again something about meat in a hidden whisper
and returned from a journey with a soul offered here and there
this steadfastly-elusive woman
again seems to act out the part of repentance
 – but something has altered the little girl's eyes – and the door will
    not close
something has long been glowing with embers of heart of the End:
    someone there
(I cannot) is living for me

1990

QUIETNESS WITH A HAPPENING

1

her islands

2

and again – it grows dark:
this is human-quietness
(how strange) without danger

3

and – (with nobody) – light

4

again – the movement
of her islands

Bochum, 1992

DRAWING LONG AGO

to N. Dronnikov

. . . first mark of the pencil
A. Tvardovsky

the match could whisper — and the candle
was a World receiving in itself — and it seemed that crumbs
in the twilight consolingly-glowed of bread
with light — going out into hearts
(. . . and why then not? . . .) — and the hand was weighted with
    quietness
ever more "visible":
the eye
as if to cool spring — falling . . . — (traces began granular
first
sliding — as if uphill!
 — . . . a rustling — His talking . . . — through us
here: with the World)

1992

PHLOXES AT NIGHT IN BERLIN

to G.A.

as if from the head
powers fall unseen!
and in that weakness called "soul"
villages-and-mist sing-shout
where suns that seem living
are sorrowful – huge – distant! –
amid their tatters
(so – a clump: as if on the edge of the Land:
I shall not call it "native":
is trembling)

1992

TWO EPILOGUES

1

cleanness of the path
simplicity of water –

and such a sky – as if a dream
of this height – unknown to all
very – oh yes very – different
bright poverty of Earth –

speaking a little to us

"while we are in the world
smoke – in cottage chimneys – plays"*

2

something hospital-dimly-white
in the field slid and shifted
 – God grant us this quietness cure us –
and the road out of the window as if beyond gates
was fading ever damper more sadly
"there" as if whispered "is all our earthly road"

1993-1994
Denisova Gorka

*These two lines, according to the great Chuvash poet Vasley Mitta (1908-1957) were sung by his father, the illiterate peasant Yagur Mitta.

DAUGHTER IN A CLEARING

a clearing. . . — and there:

a glimmer (like song):

(it is you) —

heaven looking . . . — as if the World understood it all:

"Oh, stay,

Happiness. You are complete." —

:

(field of forest clearing)

1995

BIRCH AT NOON

in the burning of noon
suddenly –

set strongly
apart
a birch –

brightly – like some new Gospel:

(self-sufficing – disturbing
no-one) –

constantly – opening out:

and leafing itself –

(all – "in God")

1995

DURING A FRIEND'S ILLNESS

for Leonard Daniltsev's painting

it seemed a dream of God — and now a memory
folding into a Vision forgotten (now falling apart now
    beginning again)
of snow on faraway hills and roads
of children's speech-clothing
of animals' faces of smile-and-weeping — close by — on the
    threshold of friends:
of you — my dears: oh, painting, life,
Recent-Inexpressible
(beautiful like a poor man's meal)

1996

FIELDS OF THIS SUMMER

to A. Kh.

and even here
time seems to tremble – again renewing
these farewell-fields –

(like peoplefarewells) –

now they stretch out like tremulous darkness
(in something ever more
earlier – than childhood) –

now – stumbling in soul's unevenness
you awaken in the grass – as in memory
someone's departedness –

(and the grasses spill out
the last speaking) –

and the rustle – the scraping (somewhere a digging
of someone underground . . . no: it is nearer:
"it is
the heart growing old") –

and then – as if they had just
opened a window
on the path –

and clouds over grasses
make a universe . . . –

they seem
to move — to rise up!
as if all this
Builds-and-Chants — the inviting Harmonious
somewhere
Breathing —

and concluding — so we too must fall silent:
"far off" — it is only a quiet sound
of a distant homeland . . . (oh yes: like a hymn. . .)
and this
is straightway
long ago

1997

DRAWING FOR PETER FRANCE

over the dusty road
there – outside – a swift
against the curtain
like the flick – of scissors

Denisova Gorka
16 July 1997

WITH AN ANCIENT MEMORY
(POEM INCLUDING MUSIC)

to Felix Philipp Ingold

as if with the neck I listen to the troubling rustle:

smoke above chimneys is made more intense
by branches invading the general garden confusion
and again – and ever more sadly – it seems
that a quietly-beautiful birth
is somewhere happening now . . . . . – (*here*
instead of the called-for name –

a few bars of the "Trout")

August 1997
Denisova Gorka

FROM LINES IN A DREAM

and with the left side of the face
looking aslant
honestly directly
the pallor – in a dream – of Shostakovich
sacrificially – crying
as through fractured mud –

as if – to a friend

7 April 1998
(before dawn)

DAY – TOWARDS EVENING

And they float out and are fixed
and settled – these Stacks
of the end – of the coming
Millennium (. . . convention of a moment. . .) – and the Setting Sun's
magnificence
steadfastly – meanwhile – abides – and soon the immortal
Seal of the Road
openly settles itself – visibly-slowly:
on the edge of the forest – for ever – to Shine

1998

LONG AGO

And in the field
sheaves were weeping – with backs
damp and golden –

leaning on the walls
of the uncut rye . . . –

dawn was breaking
and the weeping remained . . . –

the World – lay steady.

1998

BEGINNING FROM THE FIELD

all day – the wind's repetition
of itself
from the edge – of the nearby field:

visibly – lightly – widely! –

but here – among peasant
buildings
its stumbling steps
ever deeper – like a meeting
with "Someone" – of the soul! –

no clarity – no distinction

1999

THE PEOPLE ARE A TEMPLE

And souls are candles, each lighting the other.

6 January 2000
Epiphany
Village of Romashkovo

FROM "LONG PARTING"

here my brothers are walking through the light of the sun
and the walls are saying "Lord" and the fields are singing
and the oaks are warm as if the substance of gratitude
in them is as audible as speech

well already nearby there is water with no waves
and the grass has no quality of contact
the brothers flit by among the irrevocable
and for me there is no leaping into this chain

3-4 May 2002
Denisova Gorka, forest

(13-15 June, Maastricht)

SILVIA'S WORLD

Two Notes

In February 1991, when Gennady Aygi was visiting Paris, he stayed for a time with a family consisting of a mother, Louise, and a daughter, Silvia. In parting, Louise gave the poet a new notebook with a floral cover by William Morris and asked him to write a few words in it as a keepsake for Silvia. To thank Silvia for her hospitality – since she had given up her room to him—"Uncle Aygi" transformed the 32-page booklet into a book of verse, writing one phrase on each page in the 32 minutes before Silvia woke up. All this happened in Paris, in the Street of the Bankers.

F.M.
Rennes
December 1992

For a long time I did not know what had happened to Silvia and Louise, or indeed to the little book. I even asked French friends to find out about them (the more so because there was a sense of precariousness and poverty in Louise's family and my memories of them both were rather worrying). One Parisian friend went to their house and was astonished by what she found: "It's like a fairy story. In the Street of the Bankers the houses are all there, all except for that one, but where it used to be there's just empty space" (and the Street of the Bankers is in central Paris).

Then suddenly, in March of this year, when I was once again in Paris, I got a parcel through the post with two copies of the little book, beautifully printed in three languages (Russian, French and Breton). It turned out that my friend, the excellent translator André Markowicz, had published it in 1992 in Rennes, with the publishing house La Rivière Echappée. André himself had translated it into French and Alan Botrel into Breton.

So the book has been found, and I hope that in due course I will find Louise and Silvia.

Gennady Aygi
Moscow
· May 2000

*

27 February 1991
Aygi

*

so – the wind's opening word

*

knightly armor of the sun

*

morning's "why are you pushing?" of the pillow

*

puzzlement of the mirror

*

angry exclamation of the toothbrush

*

cheerful babble of soap

*

shining "all correct" of the thermometer

*

feverish humor of mineral water

*

diplomatic negotiations of wallpaper

*

blessed smile of the milk

*

vagrant "tok-tok" of the doorpost

*

journeying of beads

*

endlessly delayed visit of the bankers

*

lonely "yoohoo" of gladiolus

*

"but I'm not telling" of the wardrobe

*

Verlainean soliloquy of the sky

*

arrival of mother's fingers

*

thoughtfulness of the candle

*

unexpected grandmother of the button

*

one-act play of marmalade

*

forgetfulness of the buttercup

*

drawing lessons of the thrush

*

mother interpreter of the Lord

*

leap of the flute

*

daisy dream of the grasshopper

*

silent "hello" of the nail

*

song of the little blue jug

*

running races of the bookshelves

*

little hands of the God-Child

*

eternal "goodbye" of uncle Aygi

*

this book belongs in its entirety to Silvia de Pila

POETRY–AS–SILENCE

(NOTES)

1

Listening – in place of speaking. Even – more important than vision, than any vision (even – in imagination).

And: rustling-and-murmuring. Rustle – of the origin – already – so distant. "Mine," "my own self."

There "everything" is silence. All – long since – took their leave. Buildings are empty. Cold. The former wind, – dead. Deserted the lumber-rooms. The wind, – dead scattering – of dead flour.

Not to give way to nostalgia. For I also am *not*. . . – how could I! Too much – from spaces interrupted – from "powers" long since abolished.

All was – to finish in silence. But – *there*. In the name of all that is *there*.

Without breath – of "souls." Without – meetings.

Sleep-return. But now – to no-one. Into cold. Into namelessness. Into absence.

2

Pauses are the places of reverence: before – the Song.

3

Solitary pages of verse – seeming in reality – wind-blown.

"Truth in poetry is incandescence," – a line of verse – hanging – in the void.

4

Silence is like the "Place of God" (the place of the highest Creative Power).

"'God?' – a quotation: from God." (From a poem of mine.)
This – was, when there was – incandescence.

5

Into dampness – to the left of the road at evening. There was an epoch there – the Death of Choral Dances. Like something noiselessly gnawing – the silence of the forest. And it draws us. Into – dissolution.

6

Today's verbosity. *Things* multiply – *cataloguing* of things expands. "The epic of our times."

And: when there is not that "penny" that was counted there ("among simple folk") – "to your name."

7

In Russian poetry, strange as it may seem, the *unsaid* is most frequent in Pushkin, in the last two or three years of his life. You find more and more suspension points, sentences interrupted by lines of dots. As if he was saying: "what more is there to say," or "there's no point."

8

Yes, one must not give way to nostalgia. But to mourn the dead is a duty.

9

Alas, everything that still touches us a little is from something "exalted." But you cannot say: "A curse on it." (What of it if many words are dead. Especially – the "most meaningful ones.")

And here is something – "of that kind."

10

Simplicity is more than Power: it is weakness stronger than Power: a Miracle.

11

There are lines in my poems that are just *lines of dots*. Not "emptiness," not "nothing," – these dots – rustle (this is "the world – in itself").

12

In the days of *daggers* and *swords* – the monumentality of Shakespearean tragedy.

A knife, an axe, are meaningful – in their *visible form*. They are even – *monumental*.

The monstrous war planes of today . . . are full of petty detail, like locusts. (I am speaking of how it *looks*, their mathematically-detailed content convinces only the *mind*.)

13

Some of my lines of verse are simply *colons*.

This is a silence that is "not of me."

"Quietness of the World itself" (as far as possible, "absolute").

14

A hut, a cabin – grander than skyscrapers.

Here – I hear a cry: "Culture against civilization again."

I am simply observing.

(And in any case . . . the "riposte" is that civilizations are only short periods, fragments of a single Culture. . . – yes, "since the World Began."

And – Nerval ceaselessly wandering. Speech – of footsteps, flicker of a shape, – a shade, speech of ragged clothes – in a whirlwind.

The final "poem" is made of "one's own self."

16

There are more and more trivial things. And more and more – trivial words.

Chatter of things. Chatter of poetry.

17

No way out.

18

One famous elder was visited by another, equally famous one.

They were meeting – for the first time. They began to talk. Suddenly a cock crowed in the yard.

– So you have cocks then, father? – enquired the visitor.

– I do. And what's that to you? – answered the host, putting an end to the conversation.

19

Who finds it hard to speak? – the person who is not expected. (Poet and public.)

20

A failed monk. All the "pre-passions" (still not quieted before entering into silence) "visible for all to see" – such is the "work." Not achieving – the wished-for "purification," and all this – involuntarily.

21

A Mirror that Moves. A Baedeker in Verse.

22

And here is Wagner. "In truth the greatness of the poet is revealed most of all when he is silent, so that the unuttered word can utter itself in the silence."

23

It is to the left of the village, first the road going gently uphill and then, two versts further on – a field, not a "village" field, "no-one's"; a field "in its own right." Ruts, tussocks, old dried grasses. But . . . – I must not – here – touch it (with the "gratuitousness of prose" I would only "sully" this place for myself and would no longer catch it in a "poem"), I leave it be . . . (its rustling presence).

24

Mighty silence – of Beethoven.

25

Let us be clear: we are not talking here of *beautiful prolixity* (there is such a thing . . . – the "enchanting chatter" of great works). That is a quite different kind of art (which has never been specifically studied, unlike rhetoric).

26

Faces-fields and fields-faces.

27

Just one example of beautiful "prolixity." Dostoevsky's novels, when we recall them "abstractly," are *audible*, like the wordless music of pain (and each in its own way, in a very "specific" manner).

Perhaps this is the music of Silence.

I don't want to speak in detail of the fact that there are "inaudible" works by great writers (without music . . . and apparently also – without poetry).

There is also a "purely conceptual" *engagement*, the temptation of *intellectuality*. And so there arises: the *topicality of silence*.

perhaps
as in a monk –
emptiness – you are
deceptive? you seem washed
like a vessel . . . as I wait I believe
humbly now: and any moment
like a blessing he who prays
(long without words)
will quietly receive
a poem
 – . . . *Amen*

30

In speaking composers make drawings with their hands in the air (they see by *hearing*). In "company" musicians are wittier than poets (the latter make bad jokes, as if they were emerging to the surface from a kind of verbal amorphousness). The eloquent artist is dangerous (unlike the poet, who in any case is a "chatterer").

31

Hölderlin in his last poems: "I could say much more." It's better as it is. *Silent places* (as in ancient tragedy).

32

It's strange, we are more laconic when we are very young. As if our freshly-weighty *pains*, revealed for the first time, spoke *for themselves*, laid out "anatomically" (excluding any reflections "in this connection").

33

These walls and vaults – were sung, they were spread out – upwards – by the singing of the spirit (permeating "mathematics" also), – in "modern times" we wander – with this strange "resonance," as if we were covering it with coats (there are crowds of such people), how "unsimple" we are; sadness, evening; the city.

34

A chorister in a church choir had a fit of enthusiasm. Father T. grabbed him by the forelock and began shaking him: "Just listen to him, the songbird! Be quiet, – *it's not your affair.*"

Maybe we too – sometimes – are too much like "songbirds" with those liturgies that are so much "ours."

35

A mile-post – out in the fields. It contains "the whole world," Heaven-and-Earth, winters, autumns, springs. All the laments and voices – of the wind. The "poem" is there, in the night – among the fields.

36

In art, every kind of "post-" – is verbosity.

37

The camp poetry of V.M. It contains care for his loved ones (and beyond them – for his small distant people) – and no "litigation" with his oppressors. Perhaps it is really better so? The "peasant way." A reaction to disaster: not an excess of wailing, but rather to make up the fire, feed the children.

38

Rather than cursing the world and people, better – to be silent.

39

And my mother is silent (I am about four years old): so as to – punish me. Already she is imperiously (and unconsciously) evoking – her future: absence? – is that it? . . – (I thrash about – in the grass – without her. Since long ago.)

40

Again – rustling-and-murmuring. It is – my brother.

(In sleep the same man keeps coming to tell me that he, my brother, is not dead.)

On his fur coat there is flour-dust. And outside the window, on the trees – hoar-frost.

The rough-hewn table. Bread, beer. And – I cannot remember the words.

Only the warmth of perfect happiness, – like a "halo."

And I would have written just this: "To the Memory – of the Radiance of the face."

41

"I am in your debt, skies of Baghdad" (yes, – Mayakovsky). Soon after – will come the pistol shot. And these skies turn out to be *a sketch:* an immense panorama – of Silence.

42

But – *even so. . .* Magnificence began – immediately beyond the door into the yard: in Blizzard-to-the-Heavens, in Sun-entering-the-world-with-the-Whole-World.

43

You? . . . – one of the quietly-departing dogs. (That was your joke: "Poets are talking dogs, they differ from other dogs in nothing else.")

44

And until then – ever further – into the snows. Into naked poverty. How few things were needed. Hands – only a little more. A poem . . . – all so little, all more and more – without us – the World.

45

The "singing of words" has started to betray me. I often recall a line of Günther Eich: "This red nail will not survive the winter." God grant me – I say to myself – to creak, like rusty iron, God grant me – a "tough" old age, – precision – the most indispensable words.

46

Face

full — of grief.

Grief — there — in the "depths" of the face — surrounding
the fields. Mountains and roads disappear.

Fences

dissolve into stains. Villages.

Rays shine out as in mist.

Face

(it is "mine" — "paradisal" — Armenia)

full

of grief.

Silence.

47

Unfinished speech is more terrible than silence. "Art Thou the
one?" — asked John. Instead of a direct answer — only hints.

48

And — revive the bond — with field and with Sun (oh, Morning Sun
— damp, as if sweating!), with grasses and trees (oh, rain drops — in
rough bark! — slight shiver down the spine). It does not matter what
talking there will be. There will be — the precision — of the Word —
as if *dictated*.

49

And yet, You — to us all — remained Silent. You let us have — our
words, — like an "autonomy."

Quietness and silence (in poetry) are not the same.

Silence – is quietness with a "content," – ours.

Is there "another" silence?

"Non-being does not exist, God would not have bothered with such nonsense," says the Russian theologian Vladimir Lossky.

That concerns a Silence that is "not-ours." "Including" the quietness – with silence – of the departed. Everything – *is*.

And – we shall make no suppositions – about something "completely other."

51

and – at the sight
of this revival
of a very poor twisted shrub
in a Berlin square
suddenly
the soul begins to work
and seems transported
to Russia

52

Suddenly it seemed that this August coolness was better suited – to a parting with you. (It, this coolness, seemed to breathe-and-speak – like you-at-peace.)

53

And – they ask: *about that* too – in words?

Yes, – both silence and quietness can be *created*: by the Word alone.

And the notion emerges: "Art – of Silence."

54

And – it seems that Silence itself,
entering a pile of papers,
Itself crosses out thoughts about Itself,
striving – fusing with me –
to become:
Unique
and ever more –
Absolute

July-September 1992
Berlin